A YEAR ON THE
FARM

FIRST EDITION
Series Editor Deborah Lock; **US Senior Editor** Shannon Beatty; **Art Editor** Yamini Panwar;
Pre-Production Editor Francesca Wardell; **DTP Designer** Anita Yadav, Syed Md Farhan;
Picture Researcher Sumedha Chopra; **Managing Editor** Soma B. Chowdhury;
Managing Art Editor Ahlawat Gunjan; **Art Director** Martin Wilson;
Reading Consultant Linda Gambrell, PhD

THIS EDITION
Editorial Management by Oriel Square
Produced for DK by WonderLab Group LLC
Jennifer Emmett, Erica Green, Kate Hale, *Founders*

Editors Grace Hill Smith, Libby Romero, Maya Myers, Michaela Weglinski;
Photography Editors Kelley Miller, Annette Kiesow, Nicole DiMella;
Managing Editor Rachel Houghton; **Designers** Project Design Company;
Researcher Michelle Harris; **Copy Editor** Lori Merritt; **Indexer** Connie Binder;
Proofreader Larry Shea; **Reading Specialist** Dr. Jennifer Albro; **Curriculum Specialist** Elaine Larson

Published in the United States by DK Publishing
1745 Broadway, 20th Floor, New York, NY 10019

Copyright © 2023 Dorling Kindersley Limited
DK, a Division of Penguin Random House LLC
23 24 25 26 10 9 8 7 6 5 4 3 2 1
001-334074-July/2023

A catalog record for this book
is available from the Library of Congress.
HC ISBN: 978-0-7440-7396-6
PB ISBN: 978-0-7440-7397-3

DK books are available at special discounts when purchased in bulk for sales promotions, premiums, fundraising, or educational use. For details, contact: DK Publishing Special Markets, 1745 Broadway, 20th Floor, New York, NY 10019
SpecialSales@dk.com

Printed and bound in China

The publisher would like to thank the following for their kind permission to reproduce their images:
a=above; c=center; b=below; l=left; r=right; t=top; b/g=background

Dreamstime.com: Matthew Bowden 6bc, Dima266f 6-7, Lzf 22-23, Volodymyr Maksymchuk 8-9, 14-15, Dmitriy Praizel 9br, Milovan Radmanovac 10-11, Magdalena Ruseva 21tr, Soleg1974 1b, Alexey Stiop 28-29; **Getty Images / iStock:** JenniferPhotographyImaging 4-5; **Shutterstock.com:** GTW 19tr
Cover images: *Front:* **Shutterstock.com:** JaneHYork b, mariait

All other images © Dorling Kindersley
For more information see: www.dkimages.com

For the curious
www.dk.com

A YEAR ON THE FARM

Sue Unstead

Contents

6   Wake Up!

8   Winter

14   Spring

18   Summer

24 Fall

30 Glossary

31 Index

32 Quiz

Wake Up!

The sun peeks over
the farmyard wall.
"Cock-a-doodle dooooooo!"
cries the rooster.
The farmer wakes up.
It's time to get to work.
It's going to be a busy
year on the farm.

Winter

It is winter.
The farmer's day starts
very early in the morning.
It is still dark.
It is time to collect
some eggs.

The farmer and
her dog go out to see the
hens in the henhouse.
The farmer will take the
eggs to the market.

Now, the farmer is out on the farm in the tractor.
Chug, chug, chug ...
crunch, splash, splosh.
It is cold and
frosty outside.

Today, it is time to get the fields ready.
The tractor goes back and forth, churning up the soil.

All day, the farmer drives the tractor in the field.
It has been a very long day!
It is time to head home and put the animals to bed.

The horses are in the stable.
The noisy pigs are in their sty.
The cows are in the barn.
The rooster and the hens are in the henhouse.

Spring

It is spring.
All the animals are very
busy with their babies.
"Cluck, cluck, cluck," says
the hen.

Six fluffy balls of yellow feathers run behind her. These are her new chicks. "**Cheep–cheep**," they cry.

The farmer uses her
tractor to take hay
to the horses.
A foal is trying out
its wobbly legs.

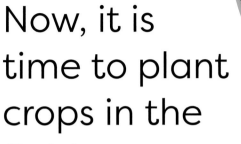

Now, it is time to plant crops in the fields: potatoes in the little field, wheat in the big field, and peas by the stream.

Summer

It is summer.
The farmer takes
her dog to the fields.
The dog will help the
farmer to round
up the sheep.

The farmer
needs
to shear
the sheep's
woolly coats.
This will keep them cool
in the summer sun.

The farmer has
lots of jobs to do.
First, she goes down
to the stream
to spray the peas.
Spit, sprit, spritzzzz.

Next, she
waters the
potatoes.
Whoosh, whoosh.
Then, she
cuts the grass
to make hay.
Chip, chop, chippety chop.

Now, it is time
to milk the cow.
"Moo," says the cow,
munching on some
tasty hay.

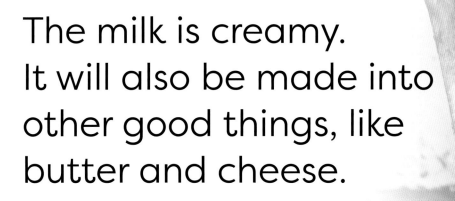

The milk is creamy.
It will also be made into
other good things, like
butter and cheese.

Fall

It is fall.
The farmer drives the tractor to the big field every day.
She checks the wheat to see if it is ready.

She picks a stalk
and rubs the grain
between her fingers.
It is time to cut
the wheat.
She goes to get the
combine harvester.

The combine and the tractor work in the field all day long.

Swish, swish.

The stalks of wheat are cut as the combine drives through them.

Whoosh, whoosh.
The seeds of grain fall
into the wagon.

Roly-poly.
The stalks are rolled into
bales of straw.

The farmer picks the apples in the orchard. The apples can be used to make yummy things, like apple pie and apple cider.

The farmer brings in a
box of potatoes and peas.
The harvest is in.
The hay is in the barn.

Zzzz.

The sun has set and
now it is time for bed.
The farmer goes to sleep.
What a busy year
on the farm!

Glossary

combine
a machine that harvests grain

foal
a baby horse

orchard
a place where fruit trees grow

stalk
the tall part of a plant

tractor
a vehicle used to turn soil and move heavy objects

Index

chicks   15

combine harvester
   25, 26

cows   13, 22

dog   9, 18

eggs   8, 9

fall   24

foal   16

hay   16, 21, 22, 29

hens   9, 13, 14

horses   13, 16

milk   22

peas   17, 20, 29

pigs   13

potatoes   17, 21, 29

rooster   6, 13

sheep   18, 19

spring   14

summer   18, 19

tractor   10, 11, 12, 16,
   24, 26

wheat   17, 24, 25, 26

winter   8

Quiz

Answer the questions to see what you have learned. Check your answers with an adult.

1. What does the tractor do?

2. What happens to the sheep's woolly coats in the summer?

3. What are two things that milk can be made into?

4. What does the farmer use to cut the wheat?

5. What are two things that apples can be made into?

1. It churns up the soil 2. The farmer shears them
3. Butter and cheese 4. A combine 5. Apple pie and apple cider